Blessed IN THE DARKNESS

STUDY GUIDE

ALSO BY JOEL OSTEEN

Blessed in the Darkness
Break Out!
Break Out! Journal
Daily Readings from Break Out!
Every Day a Friday
Every Day a Friday Journal
Daily Readings from Every Day a Friday
Fresh Start
Fresh Start Study Guide
I Declare
I Declare Personal Application Guide
The Power of I Am
The Power of I Am Journal
The Power of I Am Study Guide
Daily Readings from The Power of I Am
Think Better, Live Better
Think Better, Live Better Journal
Think Better, Live Better Study Guide
Daily Readings from Think Better, Live Better
Wake Up to Hope Devotional
(with Victoria Osteen)
You Can, You Will
You Can, You Will Journal
Daily Readings from You Can, You Will
Your Best Life Now
Scriptures and Meditations for Your Best Life Now
Daily Readings from Your Best Life Now
Your Best Life Begins Each Morning
Your Best Life Now Study Guide
Your Best Life Now for Moms
Your Best Life Now Journal
Starting Your Best Life Now

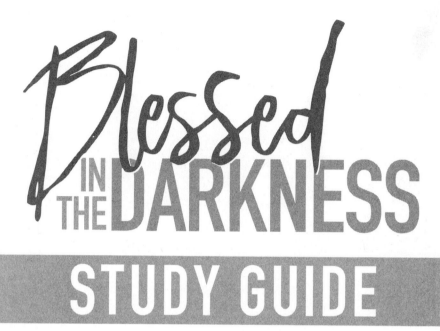

Blessed IN THE DARKNESS

STUDY GUIDE

How All Things Are Working for Your Good

#1 *New York Times* Bestselling Author

JOEL OSTEEN

FaithWords

New York • Nashville

FaithWords
Hachette Book Group
1290 Avenue of the Americas
New York, NY 10104
faithwords.com
twitter.com/faithwords

First Edition: October 2017

FaithWords is a division of Hachette Book Group, Inc.
The FaithWords name and logo are trademarks of Hachette Book Group, Inc.

The publisher is not responsible for websites (or their content) that are not owned by the publisher.

The Hachette Speakers Bureau provides a wide range of authors for speaking events. To find out more, go to www.hachettespeakersbureau.com or call (866) 376-6591.

Scripture quotations noted NIV are taken from *The Holy Bible, New International Version*® NIV®. Copyright © 1973, 1978, 1984, 2011 by Biblica, Inc.™ Used by permission. All rights reserved worldwide.

Scripture quotations noted NKJV are taken from the *New King James Version* of the Bible. Copyright © 1982 by Thomas Nelson, Inc. Used by permission. All rights reserved.

Scripture quotations noted NLT are taken from the *Holy Bible, New Living Translation*, copyright © 1996, 2004, 2007 by Tyndale House Foundation. Used by permission of Tyndale House Publishers, Inc., Carol Stream, IL 60188. All rights reserved.

Scripture quotations noted AMP are taken from *The Amplified Bible*. Copyright © 2015 by The Lockman Foundation, La Habra, CA 90631. All rights reserved. For permission to quote information visit www.lockman.org.

Scripture quotations noted AMPC are taken from *The Amplified Bible Classic Edition*. Copyright © 1954, 1958, 1962, 1964, 1965, 1987 by The Lockman Foundation, La Habra, CA 90631. All rights reserved. For permission to quote information visit www.lockman.org.

Scriptures noted TLB are taken from *The Living Bible*, copyright © 1971. Used by permission of Tyndale House Publishers, Inc., Carol Stream, IL 60188. All rights reserved.

Scriptures noted MSG are taken from *The Message*. Copyright © 1993, 1994, 1995, 1996, 2000, 2001, 2002. Used by permission of NavPress Publishing Group.

Scripture quotations noted ESV are taken from the *The Holy Bible, English Standard Version*®. Copyright © 2001 by Crossway, a publishing ministry of Good News Publishers. ESV® Text Edition: 2011. Used by permission. All rights reserved.

Literary development: Lance Wubbels Literary Services, Bloomington, Minnesota.

ISBN: 978-1-4789-7034-7

Printed in the United States of America

10 9 8 7 6 5 4 3 2 1

Contents

Introduction

We are delighted that you have chosen to use this study guide that was written as a companion to *Blessed in the Darkness*. All of us will go through dark times that we don't understand, including loss, sickness, or divorce. It's easy to get discouraged, give up on our dreams, and just settle. This study is meant to help you discover God's divine plan during difficult times.

We may not realize it, but when we feel buried in dark places, we are being blessed. God doesn't send the difficulties, but He will use those dark places to cause us to grow. We cannot reach our highest potential being in the light all the time. The dark places are all a part of His plan to make us into who we were created to be. That's where our character is developed. The thoughts and questions addressed in the following pages will help you to understand that there are seeds of talent, potential, and greatness buried deep within you that will only come to life in the darkness. As you learn to trust Him when life doesn't make sense, it's just a matter of time before you break out and blossom into your full potential.

This study guide has been created so that it lends itself to self-study or personal development as well as small-group study or discussion, say in a care group or book club setting. Whichever the purpose you have in mind, you'll find great opportunity to personally be blessed as you take time to study and meditate on God's Word.

The format of each chapter is simple and user-friendly. To get the most out of each chapter, it would be best to first read the corresponding chapter from *Blessed in the Darkness*, and then work your way through the chapter in this study guide. The majority of the questions are personal, and taking the time to read through the chapters in the book and think through how each question can affect your life will give the study immediate personal application.

If you decide to use this study guide in a small group study, a good habit is to do some preparation before each meeting. Take some time to read the relevant portions of text and to reflect on the questions and how they apply to you. This will give your group study depth and make the sessions more fruitful and productive for all.

Because of the personal nature of this study guide, if you use this study guide in a group setting, remember that confidentiality, courtesy, and mutual respect lay the foundation for a healthy group. A small group should be a safe place for all who participate. Don't let your conversations leave the small group or turn into gossip. A small group is not a place to tell others what they should have done or said or think, and it's not a place to force opinions on others. Commit yourselves to listening in love to your fellow participants, to praying for and supporting one another, to being sensitive to their perspectives, and to showing each participant the grace you would like to receive from others.

CHAPTER ONE

Blessed in the Dark Places

When we think about what it means to be "blessed," most of the time we think of the good things that have happened to us. It's easy to celebrate and have a grateful attitude when things are going our way.

1. When you think of being "blessed," what is your immediate response? Describe a time when you considered yourself as having been "blessed."

....

....

....

....

....

All of us at some point will go through a dark place.

2. Describe a time when you can look back and see God's blessings in difficult situations you didn't understand.

....

....

....

....

....

3. If you think of the dark places in relationship to the seeds of greatness in you, how does God use the dark places as a part of His divine plan?

....

....

....

....

Throughout the Scripture, every person who did something great went through one of these dark places. The dark place was a prerequisite for stepping into the fullness of their destiny, and it's a prerequisite for us as well. It's where your character is developed, where you learn to trust God and to persevere, and where your spiritual muscles are made strong.

4. What was Moses' dark place, and how did that shape his life (see Exod. 2)?

....

....

....

....

....

5. What was Esther's dark place, and how did that shape her life (see Esth. 4)?

....

....

....

....

....

6. What was Elijah's dark place, and how did that shape his life (see 1 Kings 19)?

....

....

....

....

....

It's in the dark places where you pray more, draw closer to God, and take time to get quiet and listen to what He's saying. In those dark places you reevaluate your priorities, you slow down and take time for family, and you get a new appreciation for what God has given you.

God uses the dark places. When Joseph was falsely accused and put in prison for thirteen years, the Scripture says, "He was laid in chains of iron, *and* his soul entered into the iron" (Ps. 105:18 AMPC). In that prison Joseph developed strength, a perseverance that he could not get any other way. Some lessons can only be learned in the dark places.

7. When you go through a few dark places, it toughens you up. It puts some steel in your backbone. Write out some specific ways that the dark places in your life have made you into who you are today.

> *To have no opposition, no problems, and nobody coming against you may sound good, but it will stunt your growth.*

---

8. Why should we not complain about the dark times?

King David said, "I called on the LORD in distress; the LORD answered me and set me in a broad place" (Ps. 118:5 NKJV). He didn't get enlarged in the good times; he was enlarged when things weren't going his way.

9. What was David's attitude through the dark places in the shepherds' fields?

    ....

    ....

    ....

10. Read Psalm 23:1–4. What does this tell you about where God will lead you and the role of faith you must maintain?

    ....

    ....

    ....

    ....

    ....

11. Read Psalm 23:5–6. What happens when you have gone through the dark place in the valley?

    ....

    ....

    ....

    ....

12. Why is it so important to be faithful in the dark places?

    ....

    ....

    ....

When my father went to be with the Lord in 1999, that was the greatest challenge I had ever faced—a dark place. When you go through a loss, it's easy to get discouraged and feel as though God had let you down and there will never be any more good days. But I've learned that every time something dies in my life, something else is coming to life.

13. Describe a time in your life when something looked like an end, but God brought a new beginning.

....

....

....

....

....

....

....

....

Think about this: an exclamation point is simply a question mark straightened out. If you want God to turn your question marks, the things you don't understand, into exclamation points, you have to trust Him.

14. What situations or areas of your life are you facing that involve a question mark that needs to be turned into an exclamation point?

....

....

....

....

....

....

....

15. What valuable lesson can you take from the example of my friend, the baseball player, about overcoming bad breaks and injustice?

....

....

....

....

....

When Jesus was about to feed a multitude of thousands of people, He had a little boy's lunch, just five loaves of bread and two fish (see Matt. 14 NIV). Then the Scripture says, He "gave thanks and broke the loaves," and the bread was multiplied. Notice the blessing was in the breaking. The more He broke it, the more it multiplied.

16. In those times in life when you feel broken, what is it a sign of?

> *Don't settle in the valley, don't even get comfortable in the valley, for the valley is not your home.*

....

....

....

....

....

17. If you have gone through more than your share of bad breaks, losses, and disappointments, what reasons do you have to take heart?

....

....

....

....

....

....

Jesus said, "Unless a kernel of wheat is planted in the soil and dies, it remains alone. But its death will produce many new kernels" (John 12:24 NLT). A seed's potential will never be released until it's been planted and goes through the process of germination—the outer shell breaks off and the new growth begins. That's when it will blossom and bring forth much fruit. The problem with many people is that they want the fruit, but they don't want to go through the process of being planted in the dark soil and something dying so that God can birth something new.

18. What was your immediate response to this life principle? Have you recognized that it is true in your life? In what ways do you, and in what ways have you not?

....

....

....

....

....

....

19. My challenge is that you be willing to go through the process. Write a declaration that you dare to trust God to take you through the darkness.

....

....

....

....

....

....

CHAPTER TWO

Night Seasons

There are times in all our lives when we're praying and believing, but our health isn't improving. Our finances haven't turned around. We can feel alone, forgotten, as though our situation is never going to change. It's a night season. In these night seasons, we can't see what God is doing. It doesn't look as though anything is happening, but God is working behind the scenes. He does His greatest work in the dark. We don't see anything changing. But God hasn't forgotten about us.

1. How did you feel when you read the statement, "In the dark times, when life feels unfair, you have to remind yourself that God is still in control"? What ways do you see this impacting your life?

....

....

....

....

....

....

2. After David defeated Goliath, he spent years running from King Saul. Why did God not change it?

Why was it as though the heavens were silent?

....

....

....

....

....

....

In the Scripture, Ruth lost her husband at an early age (see Ruth 1). She was devastated, heartbroken. She could have given up on life and lived in self-pity. But she understood this principle: the night seasons are not the end. The dark times are simply steps on the way to your destiny.

3. The psalmist said, "Weeping may endure for a night, but joy comes in the morning" (Ps. 30:5 NKJV). What does that tell you about your night seasons? How is that shown through the story of Ruth?

....

....

....

....

....

....

....

The Old Testament hero of faith Job went through a night season (see Job 1–2). Everything had been going great. He was happy, healthy, and successful, but out of nowhere he lost his children, his business, and his health. His whole world was turned upside down. Yet Job was a good man. He loved God. He was a person of excellence and integrity.

4. If you are in a night season now, does that mean you've done something wrong and that God is displeased with you? Explain.

....

....

....

....

> "God sends the rain on the just and the unjust."

....

....

....

Job did what many of us do in our night seasons. He focused on the problem, magnified what was wrong, and let it overwhelm him. Job said, "I, too, have been assigned months of futility, long and weary nights of misery" (Job 7:3 NLT). He was saying, "This is permanent. This is how my story ends. I've been assigned to nights of misery."

5. In Job's darkest hour, when he was the most discouraged, what did one of his friends tell him God was about to do (see Job 8:21)? What is God saying to you that He also said to Job?

    ....

    ....

    ....

    ....

    ....

6. Job not only made it through the night season, but what happened to him afterward?

    ....

    ....

    ....

    ....

    ....

7. Our thoughts about night seasons usually focus on the difficulties. What should we realize about them and focus our expectations upon?

    ....

    ....

    ....

    ....

    ....

In the dark times, it's easy to talk about the difficulties, talk about how bad life is treating us. Like Job, we tend to exaggerate our problems. All that's going to do is make you more discouraged and take your joy.

8. Instead of complaining about a night season, what is one of the best things you can say? Why is that such a powerful declaration? Write a statement using it that is directed toward one of your difficulties.

....

....

....

....

....

....

9. If you're going to magnify something, don't magnify your problems; magnify your God. How can you keep magnifying Him?

....

....

....

....

....

....

10. The psalmist said, "When darkness overtakes [the righteous], light will come bursting in" (Ps. 112:4 TLB). Where do you need to get in agreement with God and start believing this is true for you?

....

....

....

....

....

....

Maybe, as we saw in the first chapter that Moses did, you made a mistake that put you into a night season, a desert place. You're not where you thought you would be and you may wonder if you'll ever accomplish what God put in your heart. Right now, God is getting you prepared for your comeback. What He started, He's going to finish.

11. A night season is a time of testing, a time of proving, when your character is being developed. Forty years after Moses' mistake, what happened to him? What had changed about Moses?

   ....

   ....

   ....

   ....

   ....

12. Reflect upon the thought that whatever you are going through, and despite whatever mistakes you may have made, God is preparing you for where He is taking you.

   ....

   ....

   ....

   ....

   ....

In the night seasons, you need to pass the tests, change where you need to change, and deal with the areas that God is bringing to light.

13. Name an area of your life that you will prove to Him that you'll do the right thing when it's hard.

   ....

   ....

   ....

   ....

   ....

When a caterpillar is in the dark confinement of the cocoon, it doesn't realize it is undergoing a transformation into a beautiful butterfly. Similarly, we all dislike the night seasons, but it is in the dark that a transformation is taking place within us.

14. Compare the transformation of the caterpillar to the process of change that God brings through the night seasons.

....

....

....

....

....

15. What was the spiritual condition of Jacob's heart and where was he when he received his first revelation from God (see Gen. 28)? What was God showing us about Himself through Jacob's experience?

....

....

....

....

....

16. Like Jacob, you may be in a difficult place now. Where is God in relationship to you, and what is He about to do?

....

....

....

....

....

In the city of Philippi, Paul and Silas had been imprisoned in the inner dungeon, with their feet in chains (see Acts 16). But *at midnight* as they were singing praises to God, suddenly there was a great earthquake. The prison doors flung open, and the chains came off their feet. What happened? God shifted the earth, the prison doors, and the chains. It was just another night shift for the God who works the night shift.

17. The Scripture says, "God never sleeps." He doesn't just work the night shift, He shifts things in the night. What does that say about the difficulties that look permanent in your life?

....

....

....

....

18. In Genesis 2, God put Adam into a deep sleep in order to create Eve. What amazing discovery did Adam make when he woke up?

....

....

....

....

19. Why does God put us to sleep, so to speak, and have us go through a night season?

....

....

....

....

CHAPTER THREE

Secret Frustrations

Life is full of seeming contradictions that try to keep us in the darkness. You're helping other people get well, but you don't feel well. You're working just as hard as coworkers who keep getting promoted, but nobody notices you. All of us have secret frustrations—things that we know God could change. He could open the door, or remove the temptation, or give us the baby we're dreaming about, but it's not happening. It's easy to get stuck with the "why" questions.

1. What do we need to realize about God and our "why" questions?

2. The apostle Paul repeatedly implored God to take away "a thorn in the flesh." What was your immediate response to God's answer to Paul?

> *"My grace is sufficient for you, for My strength is made perfect in weakness."*

3. Is there something you've implored God to change, but nothing's improved? Describe one example from your experience and how you responded.

....

....

....

....

....

4. What is the right attitude to hold toward secret frustrations?

....

....

....

Here's a key: don't focus on the frustration.

....

....

....

If you're going to reach your full potential, you can't be a weakling. You have to be a warrior.

5. Do you see yourself as a warrior? What change in your thinking will help you improve in this area?

....

....

....

....

....

....

....

6. When Jesus healed a man who had been crippled for thirty-eight years, why did He tell him to take up his bed and walk (see John 5)? The man didn't need his bed anymore, so what purpose did the bed serve?

....

....

....

....

....

7. Even though God frees you from certain things, the temptation, the weakness, or the limitation may not totally go away. Explain why.

....

....

....

....

....

In the Old Testament, God showed Moses several signs so that he would go into the courts of Pharaoh with confidence, knowing that God was with him. But He did not take away Moses' stutter, despite Moses' request. In effect, He was saying to Moses what He said to Paul, "My strength is made perfect in your weakness."

8. If you are waiting for God to remove something from your life, but it's not happening, what will keep you from living frustrated about it?

....

....

....

....

....

The Scripture talks about how we have treasure "in earthen vessels" (2 Cor. 4:7 NKJV). Yet all of us have imperfections within our clay pot—seeming contradictions. There's something that's not being removed or changed that could easily irritate us and cause us to live frustrated.

9. What is your secret frustration? Is it stealing your joy? Write a declaration that states you're going to keep doing the right thing even when you're not seeing right results.

....

....

....

....

....

....

The Scripture says, "I have tested you in the furnace of affliction" (Isa. 48:10 NKJV). Some things you can't learn by reading a book or listening to a message. You have to experience it. That's where your spiritual muscles are developed. Character is developed in the tough times.

10. Describe a time when you were tested in "the fire of affliction." How did God use that to change your life? How did it become a blessing?

....

....

....

....

....

....

....

11. What was your immediate response to the statement that "our character is more important than our talent"? How have you found this life principle to be true in your life?

....

....

....

....

....

....

....

....

> *Can you trust Him with the secret frustrations, the things that haven't changed?*

12. For many years my father's secret frustration was that the congregation at Lakewood was not growing. What he didn't realize was that he was developing character; he was proving to God that he would be faithful in the tough times. Maybe you're doing the right thing, but your secret frustration is not changing. How do you keep from getting sour and losing your passion?

....

....

....

....

....

....

....

....

....

....

....

....

13. In the Genesis 29–30 story, what did Rachel have that Leah did not have? What was Rachel's secret frustration?

_____

_____

_____

_____

_____

14. What did Leah have that Rachel did not have? What was Leah's secret frustration?

_____

_____

_____

_____

15. Neither Rachel nor Leah could do a thing to change their secret frustrations. The same is true for each of us. What is the right attitude to have toward your secret frustration?

_____

_____

_____

_____

_____

Years later, God removed the barrenness from Rachel, and she had a remarkable son named Joseph. The darkness gave way to the light, and that secret frustration gave way to a huge blessing.

For most of my father's life, he struggled with high blood pressure even while He was faithfully serving God, helping people, changing lives all over the world. For some reason God never took it away. The last words my father ever spoke concerned the difficulties with this sickness: "I don't understand it all, but I know this: His mercy endures forever."

16. My father had a made-up mind that no matter what, he was going to stay in faith. What lesson can you adopt from his example?

....

....

....

....

....

....

....

17. The three Hebrew teenagers in Daniel 3 wouldn't bow down to the king's golden idol. Using their statement of faith to the king, write your own statement of faith that will overcome your secret frustration as well as all the forces of darkness that try to keep you from your destiny.

....

....

....

....

....

....

....

CHAPTER FOUR

Unconditional Trust

It's easy to trust God when things are going our way and life is good. But when our prayers aren't being answered, the problem isn't turning around, and we're not seeing favor, too often we get discouraged and think, *God, why aren't You doing something?* We think that when it changes, we'll be happy. "When my health improves, I'll have a good attitude." Conditional trust says, "God, if You answer my prayers in the way I want and according to my timetable, I'll be my best."

1. What is the problem with conditional trust? What is real faith?

....

....

....

....

....

....

2. Think for a moment about a past specific issue of conditional trust in your life. What outcome did it lead to?

Trust Him when you don't understand.

....

....

....

....

....

....

....

God can see things in you that you can't see in yourself. His plan for your life is bigger than your plan. But God doesn't take us in a straight line. Part of His plan involves twists, turns, disappointments, losses, and bad breaks. If you have conditional trust, you'll get discouraged and think, *Why is this happening?* But God is still directing your steps. Trust Him even when it feels as though you're going the wrong direction.

3. The loss of my father was the darkest hour of my life, yet in one sense God turned it into my brightest hour. What does that tell you about the times in your life when you feel everything is going in the wrong direction?

_____

_____

_____

_____

_____

_____

4. How have you responded to these dark times when God does not seem to be answering your prayers? How can you keep these issues where a "want" is not being fulfilled from consuming your thoughts and prayers?

_____

_____

_____

_____

_____

_____

_____

Previously I told the story of the three Hebrew teenagers who refused to bow down to the king's golden idol and declared to the king of Babylon, "We're not going to bow down. We know that our God will deliver us. But even if He doesn't, we will not bow." That's unconditional trust.

5. Write an honest review of what you think you would have said and done if you had been in one of those young men's shoes.

_____

_____

_____

_____

_____

_____

_____

_____

6. The psalmist said, "The LORD will work out his plans for my life" (Ps. 138:8 NLT). How can believing this truth take the pressure off you?

_____

_____

_____

_____

_____

_____

_____

_____

As was true of the three Hebrew teenagers, dare to trust God not just when things are going your way, but even when you don't understand it.

7. When a lot is coming against you and you feel as though you're about to be thrown into a fire, what good news can you take from their story?

> *Sometimes God's plan includes giants, Red Seas, Pharaohs, and other people who don't like you.*

8. The three Hebrew teenagers were miraculously saved. What might the outcome have been if they would have had conditional trust?

9. How does the attitude that you will continue to honor God no matter what happens to you take away all the enemy's power?

The Scripture says, "You'll not be harvested until it's time" (Job 5:26 TLB). You may get thrown into a fire, but if it's not your time to go, you're not going to go. God has the final say. Right now He is working out His plan for your life. There may be some fiery furnaces. Are you going to trust Him only if He delivers you from the fire?

10. God says, "As the heavens are higher than the earth, so are my ways higher than your ways and my thoughts than your thoughts" (Isa. 55:9 NIV). Describe a situation in your past when you realized God's plan for your life was better—more rewarding and fulfilling—than your plan.

....

....

....

....

....

....

....

The longer I live, the more I pray, "God, let not my will but Your will be done."

11. We all love it when God opens doors for us. What attitude should you have when He closes a door you wanted to stay open?

....

....

....

....

....

....

....

I believe in praying for our dreams and praying bold prayers, believing for big things. But I've learned to let God do it His way. Hold tightly to what God put in your heart, but hold loosely to how it's going to happen. Don't get set in your ways. Don't be discouraged because it hasn't happened the way you thought. God is working out His plan His way.

12. When Victoria and I went to buy our first home, the door to what we thought was our dream house closed. Have you ever felt as though God let you down when a door closed for you? Describe your experience and what you felt.

> *Let God do it His way.*

13. What was your immediate response to the statement that "the closed doors, the disappointments, the delays; it's all working for you"? What truth will you tell yourself to keep you from living frustrated?

Abraham had prayed, believed, and stood in faith for twenty-five years and finally saw God's promise come to pass in the birth of their son Isaac. You can imagine how Abraham felt many years later when God told him to take Isaac to the top of a mountain and sacrifice him (see Gen. 22). Isaac, his beloved son, was the fulfillment of the promise God had given him. Now God was asking him to put his dream on the altar. Abraham didn't understand it, but he was obedient. He passed the trust test. And just as he was about to follow through, God stopped him and said, "Don't do it. Now I can see you trust Me more than anything."

14. Like with Abraham, there will be times when God asks us to put our dream on the altar. Describe one such trust test in your life. Did you pass it? What can you learn from Abraham's experience that will help you with your future trust tests?

God will not only give you the desires of your heart, He'll do more than you ask or think.

CHAPTER FIVE

Don't Waste Your Pain

We all go through difficulties, setbacks, and loss. Pain is a part of life, and it often feels like a dark place. It's easy to get discouraged and think, *God, why did this happen to me?* But one of the most important things I've learned is not to put a question mark where God has put a period. All of us have things we don't understand. One reason is that we can't see the big picture for our lives.

1. If you take one piece of a jigsaw puzzle and isolate it, what will you think about it in regard to the entire puzzle?

    ....

    ....

    ....

    ....

2. If you take painful times in your life and isolate them, what will you think about them in regard to God's plan for your life?

    ....

    ....

    ....

    ....

3. What is the key to understanding your times of pain? How can you come out better rather than bitter?

    ....

    ....

    ....

    ....

The Scripture talks about how God is not only in control of our lives, but He's in control of the enemy. Satan had to ask for permission from God before he could test Job (see Job 1–2). The enemy may turn on the furnace, but God controls how much heat, how much pain, how much adversity we will face. He knows what we can handle. If it is going to harm us rather than help us, He dials it back.

4. You've heard the saying "No pain, no gain." What truth about God will strengthen you during times of pain? Why should you not complain about struggles and difficulties? Where is the blessing in pain?

....

....

....

....

....

....

....

5. What lesson did you take away from the experiment with honeybees aboard the space shuttle *Columbia*? How are we like the bees?

Quit telling yourself that you can't take it.

....

....

....

....

....

....

....

....

6. Write an honest review of how you typically respond to times of pain—not how you wish you responded, but your real thoughts. Perhaps use a past experience to describe your thoughts.

....

....

....

....

....

....

....

....

....

There is purpose in your pain. God allows the pain, but He doesn't say, "Let Me give them some pain or heartache to make their life miserable." He uses it for a purpose. We're not always going to understand it. "Why did…?" I can't answer the whys, but I can tell you that if God allowed it, He knows how to bring good out of it.

7. How does this perspective that there is a purpose in your pain compare to your answer to the question above? Write down the words of truth that will help keep your faith strong during these tough times.

....

....

....

....

....

....

....

Sometimes we bring pain on ourselves. We make poor choices, get in a relationship that we knew would not be good, or get in over our head in our spending, and then there is pain to deal with as a consequence.

8. In order not to waste the pain in these situations, what must you do?

....

....

....

....

....

....

9. While it is important to let go of the past—the divorce, the failure, the bad break—what do you first need to remember?

> *Don't be hardheaded and keep going through the same pain again and again.*

....

....

....

....

....

....

10. How can you keep from repeating the same painful mistakes? Write down an example that you need to correct now.

....

....

....

....

....

....

Sometimes we experience pain that has nothing to do with our choices. It isn't our fault. We're doing the right thing, and the wrong thing happens.

11. When my mother was diagnosed with terminal cancer, rather than put a question mark where God had put a period, she put her life completely into God's hands. Apply this powerful principle to whatever is worrying or stressing you. Be specific.

    ....

    ....

    ....

    ....

    ....

    ....

    ....

    ....

12. When God allows you to go through a painful season, what encouragement can you take from 2 Corinthians 1:3–4: "the God of all comfort, who comforts us in all our troubles, so that we can comfort those in any trouble with the comfort we ourselves receive from God"?

    ....

    ....

    ....

    ....

    ....

    ....

    ....

    ....

Candy Lightner was so devastated by the loss of her daughter's life to a drunken driver that she didn't think she could go on. But then something rose up in Candy that she had never felt—a mother's rage. In her late daughter's bedroom, she started an organization with no money, no influence, and no experience. She called it Mothers Against Drunk Driving (MADD). Thirty-seven years later, it is one of the country's largest activist organizations and has saved hundreds of thousands of lives, changed laws, and influenced public awareness and policy.

13. Candy didn't waste her pain. She took one of life's greatest pains and turned it around to become a force for good. What are you discovering about God that gives you the power to do the same with your pain?

....

....

....

....

....

....

14. When you've been through something, in one sense you've been given a gift. You're uniquely qualified to help somebody else in that situation. What have you gone through that you could use to help others?

Can God trust you with pain?

....

....

....

....

....

....

....

The Scripture says, "Because of the joy awaiting [Jesus], he endured the cross" (Heb. 12:2 NLT). If you just focus on the present pain, you'll get discouraged and think, *This isn't fair. I can't take it anymore.* Have a new perspective and say, "This pain is difficult, but I know this pain is not here to defeat me. It's here to promote me to something new."

15. Like the lady who didn't realize she was pregnant, there are many times when we're pregnant but we don't know it. All we feel is the pain. What is the pain a sign of? What do you need to focus on?

....

....

....

....

....

16. The Champions Club is a ministry that was birthed as a result of one couple's pain. Reflect upon how pain has birthed a blessing in your life. How was it a gift to you?

....

....

....

....

....

17. Write a big bold prayer that you will not waste your pain.

....

....

....

....

CHAPTER SIX

Blessed by Your Enemies

We all know that God can bless us, show us favor, promote us, heal us. But God can also use our enemies to bless us. That person who left you, that coworker who's trying to make you look bad, that friend who disappointed you—you couldn't reach your destiny without them. It's all a part of God's plan to get you to where you're supposed to be.

1. Goliath was Israel's number one enemy. Why was he placed strategically in David's path?

    ....

    ....

    ....

    ....

    ....

2. There are Goliaths ordained to come across your path. What do you need to understand about them?

    ....

    ....

    ....

    ....

    ....

3. What does this also tell you about your friends and associates?

    ....

    ....

    ....

    ....

    ....

When we received word that the city leaders of Houston were thinking about selling the Compaq Center, I knew it was supposed to be ours. But there was opposition to our getting the building, and in particular one high-powered business executive who said sarcastically, "It will be a cold day in hell before Lakewood gets that building."

4. That executive was one of those Goliaths whom God had strategically placed in our path. How did God use him in my life?

> *Many times your enemies will do more to catapult you to success than your friends.*

5. Has God placed a Goliath in your path in the past to stir you up and overcome a challenge? Describe it.

David said to God, "You prepare a table before me in the presence of my enemies" (Ps. 23:5 NIV). When God brings you through the dark valley of opposition, He's going to do it in such a way that all your enemies can see He has blessed you. Our building is on the second busiest freeway in the nation. Every time that executive who said we'd never get the Compaq Center drives by, I imagine he thinks, *It's a cold day in hell.*

6. What enemy are you up against at this present time? What is your perspective of it? How aligned are your thoughts to David's statement?

    ....

    ....

    ....

    ....

    ....

    ....

    ....

7. The betrayal of Jesus by Judas was perhaps the darkest betrayal in all of history. What did Jesus understand about this betrayal? What powerful lesson can you take from Jesus' response to what Judas did?

    ....

    ....

Nothing happens by accident.

    ....

    ....

    ....

    ....

    ....

There are some things that we don't like and may even be praying for God to take away from us that if He removed them, we wouldn't reach our highest potential. That opposition is making you stronger. Those people who try to push you down, the betrayal, the disappointment—none of these can keep you from your destiny. God has the final say.

8. A well-known minister said that a local newspaper's negative stories about him only made him stronger and more diligent. Write a statement of faith that you can use to be victorious in the face of opposition.

    ....

    ....

    ....

    ....

    ....

    ....

    ....

In the Scripture, four men carried a paralyzed man to see Jesus (see Mark 2). When Jesus said to the man, "Your sins have been forgiven," the religious leaders were offended and began to murmur and complain. To prove to them that He was the Son of God, He healed the man.

9. When you face criticism and others try to push you down, how should you respond in order to find the blessing that's in it?

    ....

    ....

    ....

    ....

    ....

    ....

    ....

You need to see every enemy, every adversity, every disappointment in a new light: the opposition is not there to defeat you; it's there to increase you, to make you better. Learn to thank God for your enemies.

10. How does the businessman's story of his competitor's public criticism of his faltering business reflect on how God can bless you?

....

....

....

....

....

....

....

11. In the early nineteen hundreds, cotton farmers in Alabama faced a major challenge from boll weevils. What did this devastation lead to?

....

....

....

....

....

....

....

12. Are you dealing with some boll weevils in your life right now? Dare to write and thank God for what is coming.

....

....

....

....

....

....

The Scripture says, "Don't be intimidated in any way by your enemies" (Phil. 1:28 NLT). Don't be intimidated by what somebody says, don't be intimidated by that sickness or by how big the obstacle is. You are not weak, you are not lacking, you are full of can-do power.

13. The opposing Little League baseball coach is one example of someone or something that tries to intimidate us. Describe a time when you felt intensely intimidated and how you responded.

....

....

....

....

....

14. What can you take from that story to help you when you feel intimidated by your present-day enemies and challenges?

....

....

....

Stay in faith. God will turn it around.

....

....

15. Write a declaration of faith that states you have the greatest force in the universe on your side and you will not be intimidated.

....

....

....

....

....

After the death of Joseph, the people of Israel living in Egypt increased greatly in numbers, to the point that Pharaoh feared them and put them under slave masters to oppress them. But the Scripture says, "The more they afflicted them, the more they multiplied" (Exod. 1:12 NKJV). He thought he was stopping them, but in fact he was increasing them.

16. When you find yourself under pressure, perhaps from a supervisor or unfair situation, what is happening? Why should you not be discouraged?

....

....

....

....

....

....

Jesus spent the night before He was crucified in the Garden of Gethsemane, which literally means "the place of pressing." It was an olive field. The only way to get the oil out of the olives is to press them.

17. What lessons can you draw out from Jesus' experience, from Friday through Sunday? If you are feeling the pressure of Friday, what can you be encouraged to believe is coming?

....

....

....

....

....

....

....

CHAPTER SEVEN

It's All Good

Life is full of things that we don't like—things we see as being negative, that make us think, *That was bad. It didn't work out. My prayers didn't get answered.* It's easy to get discouraged and lose our passion. But God won't allow a difficulty unless He's going to use it to push you further into your destiny. This includes closed doors, delays, the person who did you wrong, and the loan that didn't go through. God says, "It's all good. It may not feel good, but if you trust Me, I will use it for your good."

1. What was your immediate response to the statement that "it's all good"? Take some time to list some of your past disappointments and closed doors, things that you really didn't like.

    ....

    ....

    ....

    > *Keep the right perspective: it's all good.*

    ....

    ....

    ....

    ....

2. When you don't understand or like something that happens, how can you come to actually believe "it's all good"?

    ....

    ....

    ....

    ....

    ....

    ....

Some of the things that God has in your future, if He gave them to you right now, you couldn't handle them. He loves you too much to let that happen. He's developing your character, growing you up.

3. Identify that situation or person in your life that you're trying to pray away. Why are those prayers not being answered?

    ....

    ....

    ....

    ....

    ....

    ....

The apostle Paul says, "All things work together for good to those who love God" (Rom. 8:28 NKJV). He did not say some things, but *all things*. He also did not say that by themselves they would be good, but that God would bring it all together to be good.

4. Isolate a significant incident in your past that you would say at the time it happened was not good. Have you seen God bring it all together and work good out of it? Describe how that happened or what you're hoping will happen.

    ....

    ....

    ....

    ....

    ....

    ....

    ....

    ....

We celebrate Good Friday each year, but two thousand years ago on the day when Jesus was crucified, the disciples thought it was the worst day of their lives. Their dreams were shattered. The Man whom they had devoted their lives to had been crucified, was dead and buried.

5. Take a moment and put yourself into one of the disciples' places. Describe how you would have felt if someone told you this was "good."

....

....

....   *How often do we*
                                                                                                 look back and say,
....   *"It wasn't what*
                                                                                                 we thought"?
....

....

6. How would your perspective of what happened on Friday have changed if you witnessed the resurrected Christ just two days later?

....

....

....

....

....

....

7. What lesson can you take away from the pain of Good Friday?

....

....

....

....

....

When God brings all the pieces of your life together, you'll look back and say, "Those were good Fridays after all!" You didn't like it at the time, but giving your best and doing the right thing when the wrong thing was happening was developing your character, getting you prepared for the next level. You wouldn't be who you are without that difficulty.

8. Twice we tried to buy property for a new sanctuary, and both times the property was sold out from under us. Describe a past hope that led to an initial disappointment for you. How did you feel? Did it diminish your passion?

    ....

    ....

    ....

    ....

    ....

9. Write a statement of faith that closed doors and initial disappointments only mean that God has something much better in store for you.

    ....

    ....

    ....

    ....

    ....

10. Do you find yourself being unhappy when God has not answered your prayers? What change in your thinking will help you improve in this area?

    ....

    ....

    ....

    ....

    ....

After my father had successfully pastored a church for many years and given his heart and soul to help the people, questions of whether his message fit into their denominational teaching ended with him and my mother having to leave the church. Some lifelong friends never spoke to my mother again. My parents felt betrayed and discouraged. It felt like a dark, defeated Friday to leave the people they loved and cared for.

11. God opened a door to that church, then He closed it. Despite how bad it felt initially, what would my father have told you about it years later?

....

....

....

....

....

....

....

12. You may be in a Friday right now—nothing seems good about your situation. Write a list of the reasons to stay in faith. Declare them out loud and prepare to soon step into your Sunday.

....

....

....

....

....

....

> *When you're hurting and disappointed, every thought tells you, "It's not fair, God."*

....

....

....

The psalmist said, "The steps of a *good* man are ordered by the LORD" (Ps. 37:23 NKJV). If God has you there, He's ordered your steps. You may not like the delays, the inconveniences, and the unfair situations that got you there, but instead of resisting it, trying to pray it away, why don't you embrace it? Say, "God, this is where You have me right now, so I'm going to be my best. I may not like it, but I know a secret: it's all good."

13. A man was hit by a car when he was on his way to encourage hospital patients. How is it possible for something like that to be "all good"?

....

....

....

....

14. What did God use to delay the two young college students who were traveling to Kenya on a mission project? What purpose did He have in it?

....

....

....

....

....

15. Instead of getting frustrated when God sometimes inconveniences you, what do you need to remember?

....

....

....

....

After Joseph endured thirteen years of betrayals, disappointments, and lonely nights with a good attitude in an Egyptian prison, he was made the second-most powerful person in Egypt. Despite what he went through, he would tell you what he later told his brothers who had sold him into slavery: "You intended to harm me, but God intended it for good…the saving of many lives" (Gen. 50:20 NIV). It was all good.

16. You may not see it right now, but there's a blessing in the darkness. What can you draw from Joseph's confession to help you see what looks like a setback to actually be a setup to move you into your destiny? If possible, use it to apply to a situation you are struggling with now.

> God doesn't allow anything out of which He can't bring good.

CHAPTER EIGHT

Nothing Is Wasted

We put mulch on our flower beds at home that includes a fertilizer that uses manure as one of its main ingredients. It's waste, and it smells really bad. For several days after we apply it, it smells so bad that we can hardly stand to walk outside the house. But in a month or two, the smell is long gone and the plants are blooming, blossoming, filled out with lots of new growth. That fertilizer gives the plants valuable nutrients and minerals that they could not get on their own.

1. We all go through things in life that stink—the betrayal, the disappointment, the loss. We don't like what has happened; something wasn't fair. What perspective do you need to give it?

There's going to be some smelly stuff coming your way.

2. Describe a situation where you felt as though you had some fertilizer.

3. What was your response to that situation? What was your attitude? How did it help or hurt the situation?

_____

_____

_____

_____

_____

_____

4. If you feel that you've already had more than your share of stinky stuff, what encouragement can you draw from it?

_____

_____

_____

_____

_____

_____

5. How could the young lady who grew up in a very difficult home environment have viewed her situation? What made it possible for her to go on to excel?

_____

_____

_____

_____

_____

_____

_____

6. Why do some people in the same type of situation struggle through life, living defeated and always overcome by problems, while others overcome the odds, flourish, and see God's goodness in amazing ways?

....

....

....

....

....

....

....

....

....

7. Describe a difficult, dark time in your past that you now look on and can see that it propelled you forward. How did that happen? Or describe a difficult situation in your life right now and the attitude you will bring to it in order to see it turned into a blessing.

....

....

> *"This stinks, but I know a secret. It's just fertilizer."*

....

....

....

....

....

....

....

....

Joseph's brothers put him in a pit, then sold him into slavery in Egypt, where he was falsely accused of a crime and imprisoned for thirteen years. All that injustice, that stinky stuff, seemed like a waste of his life, but just as fertilizer feeds a plant nutrients and minerals, that difficult, dark season was getting Joseph prepared for the fullness of his destiny.

8. What took Joseph from the pit to the prison and all the way to the palace?

9. David said, "[God] also brought me up out of a horrible pit...has put a new song in my mouth" (Ps. 40:2–3 NKJV). When you feel that you are in a similar pit, what should you get ready for rather than settle there?

10. What happened to the man whose boss was against him? What does this say about the difference God's favor can make in your life?

Perhaps because of a mistake you made, a poor decision that got you in trouble, the accuser whispers in your ear, "You don't deserve to be blessed. It's your fault. God's not going to help you." But God doesn't waste anything. He knows how to get good out of every situation. "It" may not be good, but He can cause "it" to work for your good.

11. Jesus met a Samaritan woman who had a rough past, made many mistakes, and had gone through some stinky situations, and yet she was the first person whom He ever told that He was the Messiah. What does her story tell you about how God can use what you've been through?

_____

_____

_____

_____

_____

12. How did God not even allow the dark life of the outlaw motorcycle gang member to go to waste?

_____

_____

_____

_____

13. How does the story of Ms. Tuff demonstrate that God knows how to bring blessing out of the dark places, that nothing is wasted?

_____

_____

_____

_____

First Samuel 21 records one of the times when David was on the run from King Saul and in desperate need of a weapon. He asked a priest if he had a sword or spear he could borrow. The priest happened to have the sword of Goliath. David left that day with the sword that had been meant to defeat him, and he used that same sword to defeat others.

14. What sort of swords does God have for your future?

15. What is the story behind the Recycled Orchestra?

16. How does God make music out of the trash of our lives?

God has you in the palms of His hands. Nothing that's happened to you has been wasted. It's all a part of the plan to make you into who you were created to be. It may not have been good, but God can cause it to work out for your good. He can take the same thing that should have destroyed you and use it to propel you. No obstacle is too big. The forces for you are greater than the forces against you.

17. You may be going through a tough time, but God is going to use what you've been through to catapult you forward. Write a plan for how you will break through the darkness and rise to the top as Joseph did.

Your best days are not your yesterdays; they are still out in front of you.

CHAPTER NINE

Trouble Is Transportation

We all go through difficulties we don't understand. But God uses dark times to move us toward our destiny. Nothing happens by accident. God wouldn't allow it if it weren't going to work to your advantage. Looking back over my life, I've realized that if a door hadn't closed, a bigger door would never have opened. If those people hadn't done me wrong, I wouldn't have the experience that I need for this new challenge. Now I can see that the whole time God was directing my steps. I thought I was going backward, but the truth is that trouble was transportation; it was moving me into my destiny.

1. Describe a relationship that didn't work out and what you gained through that experience that helped you in the future.

   ....

   ....

   ....

   ....

   ....

   ....

2. Why should you not be surprised if you face extraordinary challenges?

   ....

   ....

   ....

   ....

   ....

   ....

   ....

Pharaoh's decree threatened the life of the baby Moses (see Exod. 2). Some would say that it was too bad he was born at the wrong time. Hidden in a basket among the reeds along the bank of the Nile River, Moses' life could have ended by a thousand things, but none of it was a surprise to God. None of it cancelled Moses' purpose. God has the final say. People don't determine your destiny; God does.

3. Of all the people, who discovered the baby Moses? How do you think she would have responded? What did her response lead to?

_____

_____

_____

_____

_____

4. How was trouble transportation in Moses' life? How was it instrumental in preparing him for an amazing future?

_____

_____

_____

_____

_____

5. At the time that Moses was taken away from his home and family, what do you think it felt like? What does that tell you about feelings?

_____

_____

_____

_____

_____

6. Trouble prepared Moses to lead the Israelites out of Egypt. Describe a past event or circumstance where trouble took you to the next level.

....

....

....

....

....

> *You wouldn't be who you are today without all the things you've been through.*

....

....

Exodus 13:17 says that God didn't lead the Israelites on the easiest route to the Promised Land because they were not ready for war. He had to toughen them up so they would be prepared for what He had in store.

7. What does that tell you about the troubles you are facing?

....

....

....

....

....

....

8. God was taking them to the Promised Land. Where you think that He is taking you?

....

....

....

....

....

....

Mike Ilitch is the son of immigrant parents and grew up in Detroit. His dream was to play baseball for the Detroit Tigers and was thrilled when he was offered a four-year minor league contract. But three years into his contract a major knee injury ended that dream.

9. Where did this big disappointment lead him?

10. Was your immediate response to his story that something like it could never happen to you? Describe what you're thinking.

11. Write three power thoughts to speak out loud when you think your troubles are taking you backward or that you've come to the end.

A lot of times we're trying to pray away all our troubles. But here's the key: you're not anointed from trouble, you are anointed for trouble. God says, "I have anointed [David] with my holy oil. I will steady him and make him strong. His enemies shall not outwit him...I will protect and bless him constantly and surround him with my love; he will be great because of me" (Ps. 89:20–24 TLB). It doesn't say, "I will anoint him so he doesn't have any opposition or problems." It says, "I'm anointing him for the trouble, for the sickness, for the legal problem."

12. Write out an application of the truth of this psalm that addresses your present troubles.

You're going to see God begin to connect the dots in your life.

13. A frivolous lawsuit over the plumbing in the house we had sold early in our marriage prepared me for a lawsuit sixteen years later that affected my destiny. Is there an expiration date on the blessings of learning from your troubles?

When you study the life of Joseph, you can see how every step was divinely orchestrated. If you left one step out, the others wouldn't work. If his brothers had not thrown him into the pit, he would never have been taken to Egypt as a slave and sold to Potiphar…never been falsely accused and put in prison…never met the butler and the baker and interpreted their dreams…never been called on to interpret Pharaoh's dream, which led Pharaoh to be put him in charge of the nation.

14. What looked like trouble was really the hand of God moving Joseph little by little through the darkness into his destiny. What does that tell you about God and His plan for your life?

....

....

....

....

....

....

....

15. The Scripture says, "God will deliver us from trouble" (see Ps. 34:17). Write out what it means to you that God will *deliver* or transport you from trouble.

....

....

....

....

....

....

....

....

16. Reread the remarkable story about the young lady named Victoria Arlen. What encouragement and hope can you draw from how she defied the odds and overcame one challenge after another?

....

....

....

....

....

....

> *Trapped in her motionless body, Victoria would say in her mind, "I'm a victor and not a victim."*

....

....

....

....

....

17. Some people feel trapped in their circumstances, in depression, in an addiction, in mediocrity. If you feel trapped, write out the truth that will set you free.

....

....

....

....

....

....

....

....

....

....

....

CHAPTER TEN

Dropped but Not Forgotten

We all go through situations in which life is not fair. Someone who faces a sudden job layoff or the loss of a loved one will often feel alone and forgotten, as though he'd been dropped. Some people are mistreated and taken advantage of as children, and now they deal with shame and guilt that wasn't their fault. Somebody dropped them. It's easy to get stuck in a dark place, thinking, *This is never going to change. It's my lot in life.*

1. What did you feel when you read "somebody dropped them"? Describe a situation where you were dropped and how it impacted you.

....

....

....

....

....

....

2. David knew what it felt like to be dropped by people. What good news does he tell us about God when people reject us or come against us?

> The drop is not the end of your story.

....

....

....

....

....

....

God has not forgotten about you. He has seen every lonely night, every wrong that's been done, and every person who's ever harmed you. He's a God of justice.

3. When the Israelites were being mistreated in slavery, taken advantage of by the Egyptians, what did God tell them He was going to do?

....

....

....

....

....

....

4. What causes the Creator of the universe to stop what He's doing and take action in your life?

....

....

....

....

....

....

5. God says, "See, I have engraved you on the palms of my hands" (Isa. 49:16 NIV). How can you apply that to the times when you feel dropped?

....

....

....

....

....

....

Mephibosheth was the grandson of King Saul and the son of Jonathan, destined to one day take the throne. But when he was five years old, his father and grandfather were killed in a battle. In a panic his nurse picked up Mephibosheth and took off running as fast as she could to try to save the boy's life, but in her haste she dropped him. Both of his legs were broken, and he became crippled and could no longer walk.

6. What led to Mephibosheth becoming disabled? What does that tell you about the people who may have dropped you at some point in your life?

7. Mephibosheth ended up living in Lo Debar, one of the poorest, most run-down cities of that day. While he may have felt alone and forgotten, what unlikely thing did the God of justice stir up in David's heart?

8. When you've had bad breaks and feel stuck in a dark place, what encouragement can you take away from Mephibosheth's story?

9. Mephibosheth had been hiding, living in exile, hoping that nobody
    would know he was related to King Saul. When you have felt dropped,
    have you also found yourself going into hiding? How so?

    ....

    ....

    ....

    ....

    ....

    ....

10. Summoned to the palace, how did Mephibosheth approach King
    David? What does this say about the potential toll that life's bad
    breaks can have on you?

    ....
                                                    "Mephibosheth?
    ....   *What happened*
                                                         to you?"
    ....

    ....

    ....

    ....

11. Rather than harm Mephibosheth, what did David do for him?

    ....

    ....

    ....

    ....

    ....

    ....

Maybe you feel as though you've been dropped in a way similar to Mephibosheth. Perhaps you had a bad break, lost a loved one, or weren't treated right. It would be easy to get bitter, settle there, and not expect anything good. You need to get ready, for your time is coming.

12. What happens when the King summons you to the palace?

....

....

....

....

....

....

13. You have royal blood in your veins. What does it mean that the Most High God breathed His life into you and that He's crowned you with favor and destined you to live in the palace?

....

....

....

....

....

....

14. Like Mephibosheth, if God doesn't remove the difficulty or turn it around in your life, what does He do?

....

....

....

....

....

....

15. No matter where Mephibosheth wanted to go, he couldn't get there on his own—he had to be carried. When you feel broken and can't do it on your own, how does God see you and what will He do for you?

You don't have to be strong all the time.

16. Do you have your own Lo Debar? Why won't God let you stay there?

This is a new day. Isaiah said that God will give you "beauty for ashes, the oil of joy for mourning, the garment of praise for the spirit of heaviness" (Isa. 61:3 NKJV).

17. When you're letting your circumstances and pressures weigh you down, what does God have for you?

  ....

  ....

  ....

  ....

  ....

  ....

  ....

18. God says, "Call to Me, and I will answer you, and show you great and mighty things, which you do not know" (Jer. 33:3 NKJV). How does Dr. Cho's story of calling upon God compare to your own?

> *You're going to take your seat at the King's table and see the goodness of God in amazing ways.*

CHAPTER ELEVEN

Balanced Books

In accounting, the term *balancing the books* means making up for a loss. If an account is low, when you balance the books, you add revenue to even it out. To know how much the account is behind, you have to first take all the losses, all the deficits, and total them up. Then you know how much you need to add to balance it. One definition of *balancing the books* is "to equalize, to experience no loss." When the books are balanced, nobody can tell there's ever been a loss. There is no deficit.

1. God has promised that He will balance the books of our lives. What does that mean for you?

   ....

   ....

   ....

   ....

   ....

   ....

2. To a people who had endured a severe time of persecution, the Scripture says "do not cast away your confidence, which has great reward" (Heb. 10:35 NKJV). What is this saying to you?

   ....

   ....

   ....

   ....

   ....

   ....

When I was growing up, for thirteen years we had church in a small run-down building that had been a feed store. Some people considered us second class. I would occasionally hear them making fun of us, joking about our building. They were good people, but they dismissed us, saw us as less than. In their book, we were not up to par.

3. When God gave us the Compaq Center—the premier facility in our city, in the most prestigious part of town—what was He doing for us? What does that say about what He'll do for you?

....

....

....

....

....

....

....

4. What does God do for the people in your family line who put up with injustices but never received their reward? How might that impact you?

....

....

God pays attention. He's keeping the records.

....

....

....

....

....

....

....

....

5. For 430 years the Israelites had been in slavery in Egypt. In the Exodus, what did God do to balance the books for them, so they didn't leave empty-handed (see Exod. 12:36)?

6. Like the young man who was raised in a negative environment, you may feel that you were dealt an unfair hand in life and in some way put at a disadvantage. If you do, describe how.

7. God is a God of justice. What is the good news about His record keeping of life's unfairness toward you?

Maybe a dream didn't work out, or you're raising a special needs child, or somebody walked out of a relationship with you and broke your heart. God saw the hurt, and He feels your pain. It's not the end. You may be unbalanced right now, the discouragement may be heavy, but God is going to balance your books. Payback is coming. In dark times when life doesn't seem fair, keep reminding yourself that God is a God of justice.

8. Have you ever declared that God is going to balance your books and not leave you in a place of deficit? Write a declaration now.

Every time you are tempted to worry, turn it around and thank God that payback is on the way.

9. God didn't promise that unfair things wouldn't happen to you, but He did promise He would compensate you with what you're owed. How did He do it for the lady who was suddenly divorced and did not know how she could provide for her children?

In chapter three, we saw that Leah and her sister, Rachel, were both married to Jacob. Rachel was far more beautiful, and Jacob didn't give Leah much time and attention. I'm sure that Leah felt as though she were not good enough, inferior, at a disadvantage. The Scripture says, "When the LORD saw that Leah was not loved, he enabled her to conceive, but Rachel remained childless" (Gen. 29:31 NIV). Leah went on to have six sons and a daughter before Rachel was able to have a child.

10. What was God saying to Leah?

....

....

....

....

....

11. What is God saying to you about the special favor He has for people who are at a disadvantage?

....

....

....

....

....

12. God sees every injustice, every wrong, every tear, every bad break. As our Father, how does He respond to what happens to us?

....

....

....

....

....

Isaiah 61:7 (MSG) says, "Because you got a double dose of trouble…, your inheritance in the land will be doubled and your joy go on forever." Don't complain about the trouble; that difficulty set you up for double. That bad break and disappointment may look like a setback, but God is about to balance the books. The people in your life who have been against you and have tried to hold you down are going to see you in a new light and treat you with the respect you deserve.

13. How did Pharaoh's treatment of Moses change after the last plague (see Exod. 12:32)? Why did it change?

....

....

....

....

....

....

14. Proverbs 21:1 (ESV) says, "The king's heart is a stream of water in the hand of the LORD; he turns it wherever he will." What does that say about God balancing your books with the people who don't respect you? How might that change how you relate to them now?

"When GOD approves of your life, even your enemies will end up shaking your hand" (Prov. 16:7 MSG).

....

....

....

....

....

....

....

....

....

In the Scripture, a man named Saul was the biggest enemy of the early church (see Acts 9). He went around having believers arrested and put in jail. Nobody was more opposed to the followers of Christ than him. Yet when Saul was at the point of his deepest need, God sent a Christian named Ananias to pray for Saul and speak to his need.

15. How should you treat the Sauls in your life, those who have been condescending toward you and treated you as though you are less than?

....

....

....

....

....

....

....

....

16. If you want God to balance your books, you have to be the bigger person and bless those who have cursed you. In their time of need, don't withhold your help. What might that mean for you with regard to those who haven't treated you right? Will you show them your favor?

....

....

....

....

....

....

....

....

....

CHAPTER TWELVE

Faith for the Middle

It's easy to have faith at the start. When your baby is born, or you marry that beautiful girl, or you start a business, it's exciting. It's also easy to have faith at the end. When you can see the finish line, you've fought the good fight, and now the dream is in sight. The challenge is having faith in the middle—when it's taking longer than you thought, when you don't have the funds, when the medical report isn't good.

1. God never promised that we would reach our destiny without opposition. The Scripture says, "Do not think it strange concerning the fiery trial which is to try you" (1 Pet. 4:12 NKJV). What does that mean?

2. What did God not tell Mary when He promised her a baby Who would be the Savior of the world? What does that tell you about the dream He has put in your heart?

God gave Joseph a dream about his future, planting a promise in his heart and showing him the end. What God didn't show him was the middle. Years later, when Joseph was ruling over the nation of Egypt, I can hear him saying, "God, You gave me a promise, but You didn't tell me that I would be sold into slavery, falsely accused and put in prison."

3. If Joseph were with you now, what would he tell you about the middle?

....

....

....

....

....

....

4. David was promised that he would be the king. What was he not told?

....

....

....

....

....

5. When the Compaq Center became available, I knew it was supposed to be ours, but I didn't know what we would go through to make it ours. Why does God purposely not give us all the details?

....

....

....

....

The truth is that the middle can be messy.

....

....

....

When God brought the Israelites out of slavery, He showed them their destination, the Promised Land. But in the middle God didn't abandon them. All along the way He supernaturally provided them with blessings and protected them. He was showing them and us, "I'm the God of the middle. I'm the God who will bring you through."

6. What are you in the middle of right now? Is there a Red Sea in your path? In what way do you need to exercise faith for the middle?

7. God promises, "When you go through deep waters, I will be with you" (Isa. 43:2 NLT). What is God saying to you about the waters?

8. David says, "I walk through the darkest valley" (Ps. 23:4 NIV). Join David and make a statement of faith that when things come against you and discouragement mounts, you will not settle in the middle.

Psalm 138:8 (TLB) says, "The Lord will work out His plans for my life." It doesn't say that we have to work out our plans, make things happen with our own strength, and be frustrated when they're not happening the way we thought it would. You can stay in peace, knowing that the Lord is behind the scenes working out His plans for your life.

9. In the middle, what would the following biblical characters have said? What could they not see at that time?

Joseph—

> *We walk by faith and not by sight.*

David—

Abraham—

10. When you are in the middle, feeling on your own, what is the good news? What do you need to keep doing?

11. Ephesians 6:13 (NIV) says, "Put on the full armor of God, so that when the day of evil comes, you may be able to stand your ground." What does that say about the days of darkness you will experience?

    ....

    ....

    ....

    ....

    ....

    ....

12. How did the couple who have a son who was addicted to drugs for over twenty years demonstrate what it means to have faith in the middle?

    ....

    ....

    ....

    ....

    ....

    ....

13. Drawing from that couple's example, how can you use the power of faith to apply to a specific day of trouble and opposition you are facing?

    ....

    ....

    ....

    ....

    ....

    ....

In Mark 4, Jesus said to His disciples, "Let's go to the other side of the lake," but along the way they were caught in a huge storm in the darkness of night. The winds were so strong that the disciples thought the boat was going to capsize, so they woke Jesus up. He rebuked the storm and said to the sea, "Peace, be still!" And everything calmed down.

14. Knowing there were going to be hurricane-force winds, why did He tell them to cross the lake? How is that also true of the promise He has put in your heart?

> *He's not just the God of the start, not just the God of the finish; He's the God of the middle.*

15. In the middle of that storm, why didn't Jesus wake up on His own? What does that tell you about the middle of your storms?

16. Describe one thing that you routinely get upset over that you will exercise your faith over and remain calm because you can handle it.

CHAPTER THIRTEEN

Anchored to Hope

The Scripture tells us that "we have this hope as an anchor for the soul, firm and secure" (Heb. 6:19 NIV). What's going to keep your soul in the right place, what's going to cause you to overcome challenges and reach your dreams is when you are anchored to hope. That means that no matter what you face, no matter how big the obstacle, no matter how long it's taking, you know God is still on the throne. When you are anchored to this hope, the dark storms of life can never move you.

1. Describe a time when you went through a loss or a disappointment without the anchor of hope. What was the result?

   ....

   ....

   ....

   ....

   ....

   ....

2. Describe a time when you went through a similar situation with your anchor of hope down. What difference did hope make to your faith?

> *If you pull your anchor up, you'll drift over into doubt, discouragement, and self-pity.*

   ....

   ....

   ....

   ....

   ....

   ....

   ....

3. When David was down and discouraged, what did he realize had caused him to get stuck in a dark place (see Ps. 42:5)?

4. What happens when you put your hope in your circumstances, in people, or in your career? What is the only certain source of hope?

5. The prophet Zechariah said, "Return to your fortress, you prisoners of hope;…I will restore twice as much to you" (Zech. 9:12 NIV). What does it mean to be a "prisoner of hope"? Describe a practical example from your own experience.

When God gave Abraham a promise that he and his wife, Sarah, were going to have their "very own son" (see Gen. 15), she was seventy-five years old. It was impossible. It had never happened before. Abraham could have dismissed it and thought, *I must have heard God wrong.*

6. What did Abraham do with this seeming impossibility?

> *If you'll stay anchored to hope, God will restore double what you lost.*

7. When you're tempted to think that a promise will never be fulfilled, what wisdom can you gain from Abraham's story?

8. When God puts a promise in your heart, what must you not allow other people to do?

The Scripture describes hope as the anchor of our soul. It wouldn't say "anchor" unless there was a possibility of drifting. This is what happens in life. If we don't keep our anchor down and stay full of hope, the normal currents of life will cause you to drift. Little by little we start getting negative and discouraged, and before we realize it, we're in a dark place of doubt and worry and we've lost our passion.

9. Describe one area of your life where you've struggled with drifting. What causes you to drift? Where does it take you?

....

....

....

....

....

....

....

....

....

10. Life is too short for you to go through it drifting. Write a plan for how you will keep your anchor down and keep your hope stirred up.

....

....

....

....

....

....

....

....

....

Being hopeful is about your soul being anchored to the right thing, because if you're not anchored to hope, over time you can become anchored to discouragement, bitterness, and self-pity. Being anchored to any of those things is going to keep you from your destiny.

11. Write an honest review of what you are anchored to today. Is it hope or something else? Describe its effect on your life.

....

....

....

....

....

....

....

....

12. The Scripture says, "Hope deferred makes the heart sick" (Prov. 13:12 NIV). Why is this such a serious matter? Name an area of your life where you need to hopeful.

....

....

....

....

....

....

....

....

13. Sometimes the negative thing we've been anchored to doesn't come off easily. Write a declaration of faith that you are cutting the line to any negative anchor and putting down the anchor of hope.

....

....

....

....

....

....

14. The young man named Owen faces a life-threatening disease yet keeps boldly hoping on in faith. Write a prayer that you can say each morning that reflects God's promises and keeps you anchored to hope. Make a point to declare your prayer boldly each morning.

....

....

....   *Like Owen,*
what is now
....   *your test*
will soon
....   *become your*
testimony.
....

....

....

....

....

....

CHAPTER FOURTEEN

Pushed into Your Purpose

Sometimes God will let us be uncomfortable for a dark, difficult period so He can bless us later on. He'll close a door, which we don't like and don't understand, but later on, He'll open a bigger door. He'll take us to a new level of our destiny. God is not as concerned about our comfort as He is about our purpose. There are times when He will shake things up—a friend does you wrong, the business slows, you'll lose a loved one. His goal is not to make our life miserable; He's pushing us into our purpose.

1. When God shakes things up in your life, how do you typically respond?

....

....

....

....

....

....

2. Describe a situation in your past when a closed door was a good thing. How did it demonstrate God's love for you?

....

....

....

....

....

....

Sometimes God moves people out of our life because He knows they will become a crutch and keep us from our potential. He'll cause a situation to dry up, so we'll be forced to change. When my television producer friend left, I had to get out of my comfort zone, stretch, and start doing things I never thought I could do. God used that to push me into my destiny. Even though I was uncomfortable, it was the best thing that could have happened to me. I wouldn't be who I am today if God would have answered my prayer that he stay with us.

3. Describe a situation where God led you to step into the unknown and take new steps of faith. Why was it so challenging? How did it change you and help push you into your purpose?

> *God had to shut the doors and force me to take steps of faith.*

When God told the prophet Samuel that He was going to take the throne away from King Saul because of disobedience, Samuel was so discouraged that God finally had to say to him, "How long will you mourn for Saul, since I have rejected him…?" (1 Sam. 16:1 NIV). God told Samuel, "I've found a new man named David, and I want you to go anoint him as the next king." Notice the principle: if you'll quit being discouraged over who left, the right people will show up.

4. Have you ever had God say to you, "Quit being depressed over who left your life. Quit being sour over what didn't work out"? Describe it.

....

....

....

....

....

....

Job said, "Then I thought, 'I shall die in my nest'" (Job 29:18 ESV). He was saying that he had his nest all fixed up, and life was great. But God stirred up his nest and allowed difficulties to push him into his destiny.

5. In spite of all the adversities, what did Job know and state that helped him to come out increased and wiser? When God stirs your nest, how will that same knowledge push you to new levels?

....

....

....

....

....

....

....

Steve Jobs said, "Getting fired from Apple [the company he founded and had made successful] was the best thing that could have happened to me…. It freed me to enter one of the most creative periods of my life."

6. How can you bring that same attitude to an unfair situation you are facing?

_____

_____

_____

_____

> *Moses said, "As an eagle stirs up its nest, so God will stir up His children."*

_____

_____

7. While a little baby is in the womb for nine months, for that season it's healthy. What must happen, though, when the womb is too small for the baby's continued growth and development?

_____

_____

_____

_____

_____

8. When you're being pushed and pressured, when things feel tight and have to change, what is God doing? What do you need to get ready for?

_____

_____

_____

_____

_____

When my father resigned from a denominational church he had pastored for many years, he felt rejected and betrayed and devastated. But the fact is that God was orchestrating it all. God knew my father would never reach his full potential in that limited environment. Had those people never been against him, he would never have fulfilled his destiny.

9. Why should you not be upset with the people who do you wrong, betray you, or leave you out?

....

....

....

....

....

....

10. Persecution forced Philip out of his hometown of Jerusalem (see Acts 8:1). What did it lead to?

....

....

....

....

....

....

11. Why should you not be surprised or discouraged when you are pushed out of your comfort zone?

....

....

....

....

....

....

In the Scripture, God told the apostle Paul that he was going to stand before Caesar. He was on a boat headed toward Rome when it shipwrecked off the shores of Malta. But that storm didn't stop God's plan; it was a part of God's plan. It blew Paul into his purpose. Paul ended up sharing his faith with the people on that whole island, and many were healed and came to know the Lord.

12. How will God use the winds and storms that are meant to harm you?

Every storm you went through, every bad break, and every dark, lonely season pushed you to trust God in a greater way.

13. You have to be willing to go through the process of being pushed into your purpose. What is the right perspective to take from now on?

CHAPTER FIFTEEN

Step into the Unknown

Before you were formed in your mother's womb, God laid out your life plan. He not only knows your final destination, He knows the best way to get you there. But God doesn't tell you how it's going to happen, how long it's going to take, where the funds are going to come from, or whom you're going to meet. He leads you one step at a time. If you'll trust Him and take that step into the unknown, He'll show you another step. Step-by-step, He'll lead you into your destiny.

1. Why do we struggle so much with this method, and why did God set it up this way?

   ....

   ....

   ....

   ....

   ....

2. The Scripture says, "Your word is a lamp to my feet, a light to my path" (Ps. 119:105 NIV). What is the next step that God is giving you the light to take? Will you be bold and step into the unknown?

> *In the unknown is where you'll accomplish more than you ever dreamed.*

   ....

   ....

   ....

   ....

   ....

   ....

   ....

God told Abraham to pack up his household, leave his extended family behind, and head out to a land that He was going to give him as his inheritance, but God didn't give him any details. The Scripture says, "He went out, not knowing where he was going" (Heb. 11:8 NKJV).

3. Take a moment and put yourself in Abraham's place. What do you think it was like for him to have the boldness to obey?

    ....

    ....

    ....

    ....

    ....

    ....

    ....

    ....

4. When Jesus came walking across the stormy sea in the darkness of night, Peter was the only disciple who had the courage to get out of the boat and walk on the water to Him. How has familiarity and what-ifs kept you from stepping into the unknown?

    ....

    ....

    ....

    ....

    ....

    ....

    ....

    ....

5. When you have something in front of you that seems too big and you don't think you have what it takes to do it, what is God doing?

> *For every significant accomplishment in my life, I've had to step into the unknown.*

6. In those times when God is silent and you start to think you must be off course, what do you need to keep doing?

7. When Joshua and the Israelites came to the Jordan River, there was no way for them to get across. When did the miracle happen? Why does God test our faith?

8. When we stepped into the unknown to acquire the Compaq Center, I didn't realize how challenging the process would be, but God provided one miracle after another. Describe a situation where you saw God make a way where there was no way. What was your journey like? How was your faith challenged?

_____

_____

_____

_____

_____

_____

_____

_____

_____

9. Describe a period of time when you had to trust God when He was silent, to believe He was in control when you didn't see any sign of it.

_____

_____

_____

_____

_____

_____

_____

_____

_____

10. What was your immediate response to the statement "God would rather you take a step of faith and miss it every once in a while than play it safe all the time and never make a mistake"? Why is it so important to be willing to make a mistake?

....

....

....

....

....

....

....

....

When you're in God's will, there's going to be a not-knowing factor. You're not going to know all the details about how it's going to work out or where the funds are going to come from. If you're going to reach your highest potential, you must have the boldness to step into the unknown.

11. When my brother, Paul, felt led to leave his medical practice to help us pastor the church, it didn't make sense to his mind. What did he not know at the time? What does that say to you about the times when you have what-if questions about stepping into the unknown?

....

....

....

....

....

....

....

When God asked the young Jewish lady named Esther to step into the unknown, it meant putting her life on the line for her people. In response to her what-if questions, her uncle Mordecai said, "Who knows but that you have come to the kingdom for such a time as this?"

12. What was God saying to Esther, and what was her response (see Esth. 4:16)?

....

....

....

....

....

....

....

13. Like Esther, we all have opportunities that are not going to come our way again. Write a declaration that when now-or-never moments come your way, you won't shrink back or let fear or what-ifs talk you out of them.

....

....

....

....

> *Be bold, be courageous, and step into the unknown.*

....

....

....

....

....

CHAPTER SIXTEEN

I'm Still Standing

The Scripture says, "Your Father...sends rain on the just and on the unjust" (Matt. 5:45 NKJV). No matter how good a person you are, there's going to be some rain in your life. Being a person of faith doesn't exempt you from difficulties. Jesus told a parable about a wise man who built his house on a rock. This man honored God. Another man foolishly built his house on the sand. He didn't honor God. What's interesting is that the same storm came to both people, the just and the unjust.

1. Describe a past situation where God made a way for you through the darkness when there was no way. How does that build faith in your heart for whatever you're facing today or will in the future?

If you are going through a difficult time, you need to look back and remember what God has done.

The Scripture says, "The righteous will flourish like a palm tree" (Ps. 92:12 NIV). It could have said that we'd flourish like an oak tree and have big, strong, wide branches. It could have said that we'd flourish like a pine tree and be so tall and impressive that we'd be seen for miles.

2. Why would God compare us to a palm tree? What is the palm tree designed to do, and what does that say about you?

....

....

....

....

....

....

....

....

3. When the palm tree is bent over during the hurricane, does that weaken it? What happens to you when you come out of the storm?

....

....

....

....

....

....

....

....

....

4. All three times that my friend has been bent over from cancer, he has bounced back. What do you need in order to have bounce-back on the inside? What truths do you need to build into your life?

> *No matter how hard the winds blow, they cannot defeat you.*

....

....

....

....

....

....

....

....

....

5. The couple who lost everything during Hurricane Katrina bounced back in Houston and were standing stronger and better off. Write a declaration of faith that when you go through life's storms you have bounce-back in your DNA and will come through strong and blessed.

....

....

....

....

....

....

....

....

....

....

....

....

The Scripture says, "When the enemy comes in like a flood, the Spirit of the LORD will lift up a standard against him" (Isa. 59:19 NKJV).

6. List three situations where you have felt overwhelmed by life's floods.

....

....

....

....

....

....

....

....

....

7. The next time the enemy comes in like a flood, what can you expect that God will do for you? How can you have a warrior mentality?

....

....

....

....

....

....

....

....

....

....

8. What was David's biggest disappointment, biggest defeat?

....

....

....

....

....

....

....

9. When David was deeply distressed, the Scripture says, "David felt strengthened and encouraged in the LORD his God" (1 Sam. 30:6 AMP). In your own words, how would you encourage yourself in the Lord?

....

....

....

....

....

....

....

10. How do you stand up to the enemy and go after what belongs to you?

....

....

....

....

....

....

....

11. When you're in a tough time, what alternative do you have to letting it crush you and finish you off?

....

....

....

....

....

....

Psalm 18:39 (NKJV) says, "You have armed me with strength for the battle." I've found that the more difficult the battle, the more strength you'll have. Your strength will always match what you're up against.

12. Are you letting something defeat you because you don't think you have the strength to endure and overcome it? Apply the powerful truth of Psalm 18:39 to whatever is defeating you and holding your back.

....

....

....

....

> *God will help you do what you can't.*

....

....

....

....

....

....

....

....

CHAPTER SEVENTEEN

Remember Your Dream

Life has a way of pushing our dreams down. They can become buried under discouragement, past mistakes, rejection, divorce, failure, and negative voices. It's easy to settle for mediocrity when we have all this potential buried inside. But just because you gave up doesn't mean God gave up. Your dream may be buried in a dark place, but the good news is, it's still alive. It's not too late to see it come to pass.

1. What is the key to reaching your destiny when your dream is buried in a dark place?

    ....

    ....

    ....

    ....

    ....

2. The Scripture calls your dreams "the secret petitions of your heart" (Ps. 37:4 AMPC). What are the dreams that God has put in your heart? Have you pushed them down for some reason?

    ....

    ....

    ....

    ....

    ....

    ....

    ....

    ....

There are dreams in you so big that you can't accomplish them on your own. It's going to take you connecting with your Creator, believing that you're a person of destiny, knowing that God is directing your steps.

3. The enemy would love for you to keep your dream buried and convince you that it's never going to happen. How can you keep from putting more dirt on it?

....

....

....

....

....

....

....

....

4. What can use as a shovel to start removing the dirt that has buried your dream? What do you need to believe, to remember, and to say out loud?

....

....

....

....

> *God is moved by your faith, not your doubts, discouragement, or complaining.*

....

....

....

....

....

....

5. God put a dream into Caleb's heart for the people of Israel to go into the Promised Land at once, but his dream was buried because of the other people. How does Caleb demonstrate the true mark of a champion (see Josh. 14:12)?

....

....

....

....

....

....

6. What is God saying to you through Caleb's example about your dreams that didn't work out in the past?

....

....

....

....

....

7. As with Jeremiah, are there some dreams shut up on the inside of you that are like a fire (see Jer. 20:9)? What good news can you take from Joel 2:25?

....

....

....

....

....

....

Joseph had a dream that offended his brothers. If he had been content to accept the status quo and be average, they would not have been upset.

8. When you have a dream, what should you expect from other people?

....

....   *Don't waste*
                                                                                                    your time
....   *looking at what*
                                                                                                    everybody else
....   *is doing.*

....

....

9. Joseph's brothers tried to push his dream down. When you have shared your dreams with those closest to you, how have they responded? Do you need their approval?

....

....

....

....

....

....

10. When the enemy targets you with opposition because you have a dream, what is the key to reaching your full potential? What encouragement can you take from the fact that you're being opposed?

....

....

....

....

....

....

When you're a dreamer, you're dangerous to the enemy. He knows that you're headed for new levels and coming into abundance, into overflow. And he knows that there's nothing he can do to stop you. But he'll work overtime to try to convince you to settle where you are.

11. When negative things happen to you, what principle do you need to remember?

   ....

   ....

   ....

   ....

   ....

12. When Joseph's dream was fulfilled, what did he not remember and what did he remember (see Gen. 42:9)? What ultimately happened to all the harm his brothers meant for him?

   ....

   ....

   ....

   ....

   ....

13. In the tough times when your dreams are not working out, what can you take from Joseph's story to help you endure?

   ....

   ....

   ....

   ....

   ....

14. The psalmist wrote of "passing through the Valley of Weeping" (Ps. 84:6 AMP). What does that tell you about opposition to your dreams?

....

....

....

....

....

....

....

....

The Scripture says, "For our light affliction, which is but for a moment, is working for us a far more exceeding and eternal weight of glory" (2 Cor. 4:17 NKJV).

15. The next time that you face opposition to one of your dreams, describe how you will find the strength to overcome what seems like too much. Write a plan of action.

....

....

....

....

Dreams you've buried are coming back to life.

....

....

....

....

....

CHAPTER EIGHTEEN

An Expected End

This is what God has done for each of us. The prophet Isaiah said that God declares "the end from the beginning" (Isa. 46:10 NKJV). When God planned out your life, He started with your final scene. He started with where He wants you to end up, and then He worked backward. Jeremiah 29:11 (KJV) says that God's plans for you "are for peace, and not of evil, to give you an expected end." Your end has already been established.

1. Where do you end? What difference does knowing that make in how you live today?

....

....

....

....

....

....

2. Like in a movie, there will be twists and turns in your life that don't make sense. What do you need to realize about them?

God knows how to weave it all together.

....

....

....

....

....

....

God destined Joseph to become a leader in Egypt so he could help his family and the world in a time of widespread famine. That was the end. But his story took on several unusually dark twists.

3. What was the real test of faith that Joseph faced...and we face?

    ....

    ....

    ....

    ....

    ....

4. If Joseph were to talk with you today, what would he tell you?

    ....

    ....

    ....

    ....

    ....

5. What was your immediate response to the statement about reaching your destiny, "The only thing that can stop you is you"? What do you need to say when everything that is happening says just the opposite?

    ....

    ....

    ....

    ....

    ....

    ....

    ....

6. I've heard it said that God always ends in "all is well." If all is not well, that means it's not the end. Write out an application of this principle to a specific area of your life where it's not well today.

....

....

....

....

....

....

7. The Scripture says, "For the LORD of hosts has purposed, and who will annul it?" (Isa. 14:27 NKJV). What does that say to you about detours, dead ends, and setbacks you have faced and will face in the future?

....

....

....

....

....

....

8. Write a declaration of thanks to the "God who always leads us in triumph" (2 Cor. 2:14 NKJV).

....

....

....

....

....

....

How you start is not important. Don't let what you think is a bad break or a disadvantage cause you to say, "If I'd had a better childhood, if I didn't have this dysfunction, I could do something great." That's where you started, but that's not where you're going to finish. That's just one scene. What matters is the expected end.

9. How is this principle reflected in the story of the eleven-year-old boy who was left standing on a street corner?

_____

_____

_____

_____

_____

_____

_____

10. The apostle Paul said that God will bring you "to a flourishing finish" (Phil. 1:6 MSG). For God to take you further than you've imagined, what do you envision a flourishing finish looking like for you?

_____

_____

_____

_____

_____

> *He didn't say "to a defeated finish," "an unfair finish," "a lonely finish," or a "bankrupt finish."*

_____

_____

_____

11. Nearly overnight Job's life went from being seemingly perfect to being shattered by great personal losses and covered in darkness. He could have given up on life and his faith. But in the midst of the difficulty, when everything was going wrong, what did he say (see Job 19:25)? What was he saying in effect?

12. Scripture says that "after this, Job lived a hundred and forty years" (Job 42:16 NIV). When you go through a difficulty, what does the "after this" tell you?

13. What limitations are there to how much Satan can test you? What encouragement do you draw from that?

14. The Scripture says, "For the joy set before him [Jesus] endured the cross, scorning its shame" (Heb. 12:2 NIV). What joy was set before Him? What did He know that gave Him strength to triumph over death?

> *"You can destroy this temple, but in three days I will raise it up."*

_____

_____

_____

_____

_____

_____

_____

_____

_____

15. In the light of Jesus' example, dare to declare "My final scene has not been shot. I know that another scene is coming—a scene of victory, a scene of promotion, a scene of breakthrough, a scene of restoration." Write it here, and how you will stay in faith and keep honoring God.

_____

_____

_____

_____

_____

_____

_____

_____

_____

_____

_____